Anonymus

Olympian leaves

Anonymus

Olympian leaves

ISBN/EAN: 9783742875648

Manufactured in Europe, USA, Canada, Australia, Japa

Cover: Foto ©Andreas Hilbeck / pixelio.de

Manufactured and distributed by brebook publishing software
(www.brebook.com)

Anonymus

Olympian leaves

OLYMPIAN LEAVES

NEW BRIGHTON 1881

OLYMPIAN

LEAVES.

NEW BRIGHTON,

1881.

A TRANSATLANTIC EPISODE.

Her eyes were brown, her hair was dark—
You can see her daily in Central Park.
She was nothing remarkable in figure or face,
Only cheerfully bright, and wore beautiful lace.

She had many "winning wiles"
And countless "sunny smiles"
   In reserve.
She was a discriminating coquette,
And by no means cared to cast her net
   In every one's preserve.

He had a frank and trusting nature—
   He came from the land of sugar-canes.
They were different in every feature;
   And yet they were both Americans.

He never had flirted—he never could;
She *always* had flirted—and *always* would.
He thought she was perfect—he loved an ideal;
How little he knew what her heart could feel!

Venice was the town they met in,

.   .   .   .   .

'Twas in the lovely month of June;
They listened to the rhythmic tune
 Of the song of the gondolier;
They took some long and winding walks,
And had those sweetly whispered talks
 Which to him had grown daily more dear.

Their gondola floated gently, gently,
The dying sun tinged all with gold;
The deep rich tints grew fainter, fainter,
Till sombre dusk would all enfold.

Said he, " Have you no love, no life to give me
After all these weeks of hope and pain?
Is it 'cause you yourself are heartless,
That you another's heart enchain?"

She said, " I do not understand you quite.
This setting sun is just a perfect sight;
Just see that beautiful deep-tinted light
On yonder castle of the Nun,
And look, how gradually the waters bright
Are touched by rays from the sinking sun."

A TRANSATLANTIC EPISODE.

" My friend, where is your cherished, long-loved
        moral code?
    Are you sure you never flirted?" he sighed.
    " Oh! yes—I never would," she cried;
" Yet I love a transatlantic episode."

The sunlight from his heart and Venice fled
As he looked up and simply said,
                " Farewell."

THE PLEASURES AND ADVANTAGES OF SINGLE BLESSEDNESS.

I AM what is generally termed an old maid; that is to say, fifteen or sixteen years have passed over my head since I reached the marriageable age.

I am an old maid from choice, not from necessity. Any one can tell you who knew me in my youth (I may say it now without vanity) that I was quite handsome, not stupid, and rich enough to make my good qualities of some effect. No, indeed, it was not for want of asking that I never married. Why, there was young Noodle-dums, who declared he would drown himself if I refused him; but I told him that if he was so weak-minded as that he had better do so, for I certainly did not want a husband who would drown himself on the slightest provocation. He didn't do it, however, but I don't think his present wife would have been sorry if he had.

Then there was Bobby Peachum, who had plenty of money, carriage and horses, and was always ready for a

"Single Blessedness"—Bobby Peachum.

spree. But he was so fond of his dinner, and he did talk such slang. Actually when he proposed these were his words: "I say, you're a bully little girl; now just hitch on and come along with me. I'll feed you on candy to keep you sweet, and you can have all the busting fine dresses you want." I thanked him kindly, but declined to hitch on. I heard afterwards that he remarked, "There are as good fish in the sea as ever were caught."

Then there were several good but uninteresting youths who would have made most exemplary husbands, but I should have been bored to death before five months had passed.

Then there was a young clergyman, who if he had been anything else I might have married, though it is doubtful. But I did not think I was calculated for poor-visiting, sewing societies, Bible classes, etc., and I told him so, though it hurt me to see him feel so badly. I am afraid if I continued the list you might think I was drawing on my imagination. But I just wanted to show you that I have had as many offers as most girls.

And now I should like to show you some few of the advantages of my present condition. In the first place, I am my own mistress. When I want to do anything there is no one to say, "My dear, I'd rather you wouldn't" (meaning "you can't"). No one to say, if anything goes a little wrong, "My dear wife, I wish you could manage

"SINGLE BLESSEDNESS—THE YOUNG CLERGYMAN."

things a little better." I speak from what I have seen of
my sister's wedded experience; yet she has what is called
a model husband. If I had to have a man following after
me wherever I went, giving me advice on all occasions,
who would rather I shouldn't do this, that, or the other,
I should soon go round as a lunatic, and imagine the
keeper was my husband. The best of them expect you
not to lift a finger without their gracious permission.
The mere fact of having some one to tyrannize over com-
pletely makes them tyrants.

I do love children,—but my sister's children are all-suf-
ficient for me. Fancy the responsibility of half a dozen of
your own; to see that they are properly fed, washed,
and clothed; to attend to their coughs and colds; to tie
up bloody fingers, plaster broken heads, see them through
measles, whooping-cough, scarlet-fever, and other neces-
sary plagues! I am content to enjoy other people's
children without the responsibility.

I know two young married women with little babies
who think marriage the finest thing in the world. But
they, poor things, married so young that they never knew
the delights of freedom, and consequently do not miss
their independence.

Then there are some women of such soft and clinging
dispositions that a state of dependence is an absolute
necessity. They require some one to advise them in

"SINGLE BLESSEDNESS"—YOUNG NOODLUMS.

"Single Blessedness"—Young Noodlums.

"SINGLE BLESSEDNESS"—MY ADVICE.

everything, to tell them just what to do, or they would never do anything. Let such get married, by all means.

But to women of independent character, not of a domestic turn of mind, and who are capable of managing their own affairs, my advice is to join the noble army of old maids and fly the banner of freedom and independence.

THE GERMAN.

My dress is on the bed,—a cloud of blue and white,—my maid is arranging my hair in a most becoming manner, and yet I am anything but happy, and if it were not for the fear of spoiling my eyes, would have a good cry. Alas! I have no partner for the german. Oh, the horror of the thing! Will I have to sit alone, or will some one take pity on me? These questions have been revolving in my mind ever since the invitations for Carrie's party have been given out.

My family are tired of hearing the same cry, and Fred said to me at dinner, "For heaven's sake, stop that tune of 'german'! It seems to me, any way, it is about time for you to give up going out."

Time for me to give up going out, indeed! Brothers are so rude! And to make it worse, mamma does nothing but tell how when she was a girl that *she never* went to a party without having nine or ten offers for the "german," and *always two bouquets!*

Hush! there is the bell!

I thought perhaps Dick Moffat might write and ask me
to dance.

"A note for me, Mary?"

What a nice hand he writes! Yes, here it is: "May I
have the pleasure of"—but there is something familiar
about this paper—I hear a laugh, and catch sight of
Fred's laughing face behind the door. "Very clever!" I
cry out. "Dick is the last person I should expect to ask
me, so I am not at all fooled." Nevertheless I could cry
from disappointment as Fred saunters away delighted
with the success of his joke.

I don't see *why* boys are so cruel.

We are in the dressing-room at last, where I am surrounded by the girls with the same cry, "Have you a
partner for the german?"

"None of us have," whispered Mamie Anderson, my
dearest friend, "except Nina, and she is going to dance
with Mr. Black—so mean in her! You know he used to
be devoted to me, and she ran after him until she got him
for herself. He has sent her the *loveliest flowers!* O
Nina, are you going down now?" And off they go arm
in arm!

"Well, I have done my best to get you a partner," says
a large mamma on my right to her daughter as she pulls
out her dress. "I have told your brother to try and get

some one to dance with you," and they disappeared down
the stairs.

At last we enter the room. Most of the men stand
about the door; one or two have had courage to launch
themselves on the sea of petticoats.

I see Dick Moffat at the door. I call up my prettiest
smile and cast a glance at him that would melt a stone,
but to no purpose. The time glides by. I have no partner. By looking around the room you can tell pretty
much who has and who has not. When you see a girl
move her fan with a quick, impatient movement, and her
eyes go roving around the room, you may know that she
is partnerless; but let the magic word be spoken, and she
becomes calm at once, leans back in her chair, and sur-
veys the world with a smile.

I have wasted half an hour on the stairs talking to Mr.
Robinson, and just as I think I've got him up to the point,
and am about to be rewarded for my pains, I find he is
engaged for the "german"! I hurry back to the ball-
room in time to meet Mamie Anderson on Dick Moffat's
arm. *She* has captured him then for the "german"! It
is too much! And I had told her I hoped he would ask
me! Horrid thing! My eyes fill with tears.

The music starts up and the german is about to begin.
Is it a wonder we New York girls look old before our
time, when we have to go through such moments as

these? But hope springs within my breast as Carrie comes towards me with a man, a *very young* man—in my heart I know he cannot be twenty—but I meet him with a smile, and at last I have a partner for the german! As we go through the crowd I catch sight of the mamma whom I met in the dressing-room. Her daughter is standing near and still partnerless, though her brothers have done their best, judging from the very warm appearance of two young men who are trying to soothe her. I pass on, no pity in my breast. I have grown hardened to such sights in the service of the world.

As I lean my tired head back in the dark corner of the carriage, and pull my torn dress from under Fred's heels, I wonder if there are germans in heaven, and if there are men enough to go around!!

LOVE'S SPRINGTIDE.

Under trees with blossoms laden,
   Happy wander youth and maiden,
While the robins sweetly sing.
   All things blooming for their pleasure
As they stroll along at leisure,
   In the fresh sweet morn of spring.

Just for them the sky is beaming,
   Just for them the sunlight streaming,
Through the leafy bower above.
   Blossoms made for their destroying,
All things but for their enjoying
   In the Springtide of their love.

LOVE'S SPRINGTIDE.

A LEGEND.

I WAS told in the days of my childhood
   As I stood at my nurse's knee,
That over the dark blue ocean
   A ship was sailing to me.

It would come from some beautiful country,
   From the realm of some mighty king,
Whose subjects were rich from the cradle
   And never had need of a thing.

It was laden with jewels and treasures,
   With pearls and diamonds and gold;
And whatever my heart could desire
   This vessel would have in its hold.

But none could tell when it was coming,
   If its trip should be long or short,
Or the date of its shipping its cargo
   To sail from that beautiful port.

A Legend.

But some day, sooner or later,
  The ship would certainly sail,
And so I must watch for it always
  And not let my patience fail.

As a child I believed the legend,
  And oft while at play on the sand
I would stop and look over the ocean
  To discover that beautiful land.

And when far away in the offing
  I would see a gallant mast,
With childish joy I would fancy
  That my ship had come home at last.

And oft in the summer evenings
  When the fishing-smacks came home,
I'd go down to the beach and watch them
  Come in o'er the sparkling foam.

And I'd ask the kind old fishermen
  If in sailing far out at sea
They had seen a beautiful vessel
  Laden with treasures for me;

A noble, splendid vessel
  With flags and pennants gay.
But, alas! they had never seen it,
  And sadly I'd turn away.

And now my hair is silver
  That once was a ruddy gold,
And the happy days of childhood
  Have become a tale that is told.

And the dear old childish legend,
  That once seemed to me so true,
Gives place to a sweet reality
  That out of the legend grew.

For is not my vessel the future,
  That daily comes nearer to me,
And the beautiful heaven beyond it
  That far-away land o'er the sea?

Ah yes! and my vessel sails surely,
  Each day makes the voyage more short,
And soon will I anchor forever
  Safe at home in that heavenly port.

A FIRESIDE REVERIE.

THE fire is brightly burning in the old grate, before which so many nights now I have sat and dreamed of days gone by.

I was young once. It seems queer to say so now, but I really was. Many's the time this old hearth has been surrounded by my dear friends, but somehow I always liked it best when they were all gone and left me alone, or with my dearest of all friends, who could sympathize with and see in the glowing coals just the pictures I saw, and experienced the same pleasure in them that I did. But he is gone now these many years, and I always sit in the evening here alone, for people don't think much of an old woman's society at any time, and what do they care about my fire-pictures? Gracious me! What a trouble one's eye-glasses are! how many times they get blurred while I am looking down into that bright red hole in the very centre of the grate. But then my eyes lately have had a great fashion of crying when I really don't know they are. Rather nonsensical, isn't it? Brighten up, old eyes, there's my favorite picture.

An old house stands on the side of a hill. Leading up to
it is a broad carriage-road, shaded by solemn-looking old
trees through which the light shines in bright patches on
the road. It is early spring; the tender young leaves
glisten with a soft pale green, the birds are singing in the
boughs overhead, and going along the road is a maiden
beside whom a tall young man is walking and saying
something which evidently pleases her, for there is a
happy smile in her eyes as she looks shyly up at him from
under her long black lashes.

Bless me! What a start that lump of coal gave me!
It has broken in two. There's an end of that picture, and
I can't bring it back again to save myself. Oh! but this is
nice; I see another, and how lovely everything and every
one in it is looking!

A large hall filled with a gay, rapidly moving throng.
On one side is a staircase; now every one's eyes are di-
rected towards it, for on the turning, just passing the old
clock, is the same girl whom I just saw walking in the
garden, and by her side the same cavalier. But where are
they going to, and why are they dressed so gorgeously?
Down they come, her long dress of white gleaming brightly as they pass the window on the stairs, and again she lifts
her eyes to his and smiles brightly as they pass through
the hall and into a large room beyond, where stands an
elderly man in flowing white garments who turns toward

A FIRESIDE REVERIE.

them and— Oh, pshaw! Why don't lovely things last longer in this world! If I could only have seen the rest of that picture! That fire needs a poke, or else I know I shan't be able to see another. Yes, I thought that would bring it. How quiet everything is, and what a pretty bedroom. There is a fire in it beside which stands a pretty wooden cradle with delicate lace curtains, and a sweet-faced woman looks from it to the clock; the clock hands are almost on the hour; there, now they are quite. The door is softly opened and a young man enters; surely I have seen his face before, and hers too. They are the very same couple I just saw coming down the stairs.

That picture has gone too now, but it has left another in its place. The tears come into my eyes again as I look, and those tiresome glasses have to be wiped once more.

A middle-aged woman stands in the centre of a room, bending over the still white face of a man. Three workmen are in the corner by the door, their hats in their hands, and eyes riveted on the floor as if they were fairly looking through it. Suddenly the tall figure of the woman sways a little, and finally falls forward with a low cry across the body of the man. The workmen open the door softly and walk out; a ray of sunlight streams in through the window on the stairs in the hall, and I am startled again to find they are the same as in all the other pictures.

My eyes refuse to see more; besides it is late; and I
jump up and meet my own face in the mirror over the fire-
place.   It is that of the woman I have seen in all my fire-
pictures, only now it looks much older and is alone, and I
may look in vain to see the other loving face beside it.

COULEUR DE ROSE.

THEY had wandered away from the farm-house
　　That happy afternoon,
Up on the hill to the orchard,
　　That was covered now with bloom ;

Where the trees were bowing and bending,
　　With their clusters of rosy white,
And below the moss-grown carpet
　　Was strewn with the petals light.

But climbing the hill was tiring,
　　And the day was warm for a walk,
So under the bright May blossoms
　　They would rest awhile and talk.

Below them the little valley
　　Lay clothed in its robes of green,
And the softly winding river
　　Like a silver streak was seen.

Was it the smell of the blossoms
  That made the air so sweet?
Or the perfume of orchard violets
  That clustered around their feet?

Was it the bee's dull humming,
  Overhead in the trees,
That sounded so like music
  Borne on the summer breeze?

Why was the distance so charming,
  The sky above so blue?
Why the whole earth so lovely
  That afternoon to those two?

Was it the words he uttered
  As he looked in her eyes so brown?
Was it the answer she gave him
  From those same eyes looking down?

We will not ask the question
  From the story as it goes,
But perhaps we can guess the reason
  Why the world was "couleur de rose."

COULEUR DE ROSE.

THE ENCHANTED MOSQUITO.

ONCE a fairy and two imps named Green Eyes and Long Chin were rocking in a water-lily, and after they had enjoyed the gentle motion for a while they wanted something more exciting.

"What shall we do?" said the fairy. "Suppose we change a frog into a beautiful maiden!"

"Pooh!" exclaimed Green Eyes, "that's too old; let's do something fresh."

"All right," said Long Chin; "let's glide down the stream and cheat those boys fishing on the bank."

"Nonsense!" said Green Eyes scornfully; "any crab can do that. Oh, I say, here's fun! Here comes a mosquito; let's enchant him."

"Done!" cried Long Chin. (You couldn't have heard him, but it made the lily tremble all over.) "That's something like."

"Don't change him into a boy," cried the fairy, who was tender-hearted and thought that mosquitoes were bad enough already. The imps did not reply, for just then the mosquito hovered over their heads.

" Squirr-rum-boob-da-fa-teesh !" muttered Long Chin,
which magic word meant, " Monster, be thy song doubly
shrill, and thy bill sharpened and lengthened, until thou
becomest a terror to all the inhabitants of the earth !"

" Squiss-mug-wizz !" hissed Green Eyes, meaning, " Man-
kind shall be helpless before thee. Thou shalt live forever !"

The fairy just had time to wave her wand and say,
" But thou and thy sons and thy sons' sons shall not
sting," and off flew the enchanted mosquito.

" You've spoilt everything !" cried the imps angrily.
But the fairy laughed so sweetly and looked so bright
and airy as she sat there then that they begged her par-
don instantly. Wonderful to say, never since that summer
has any male mosquito attempted to sting. The fairy's
spell is upon them all. They may feed upon flowers and
such things, but human flesh *never !* Look out for Ma-
dame Mosquito though ! She lives upon blood and grows
fiercer and fiercer every year. And if any one ever meets
the Enchanted Mosquito himself, with his queer body and
long bill and tremendous song, what good is there in
being at all alarmed ? He is perfectly harmless, so don't
attempt to kill him, for it is useless to overcome that terri-
ble " Squiss-mug-wizz ! ! !"